The Cellar Dreamer

The Cellar Dreamer

Valerie Coulton

Apogee Press

Berkeley · California

2007

Grateful acknowledgement is made to the editors of *A Magazine of Paragraphs, Big Ugly Review, Bird Dog, Fourteen Hills,* and *Parthenon West Review* in which some of these pieces first appeared.

Deepest gratitude to Laynie Brown, Phillip Calderwood, Stephen Hemenway, Miriam Pirone, Monica Regan, Elizabeth Robinson, and Laura Walker. Inexpressible thanks to Edward Smallfield for the loan of a title, and for everything else.

Many thanks to Susanne Dyckman for her work on this book and for her many other contributions to Apogee Press.

Book design by Philip Krayna Design, Berkeley, CA.
www.pkdesign.net

Cover: René Magritte, *The Red Model* 1934. ©2007 C. Herscovici / Artists Rights Society (ARS), New York. Collection: Museum Boijmans Van Beuningen, Rotterdam.

ISBN 0-9787667-1-7. Library of Congress Control Number: 2006937640.

Published by Apogee Press
Post Office Box 8177
Berkeley, CA 94707-8177
www.apogeepress.com

Table of Contents

The cellar dreamer knows that the walls of the cellar are buried walls…walls that have the entire earth behind them.

—GASTON BACHELARD, *The Poetics of Space*

some where

for my parents

song's longing:
          hours
scattering
feed—the seeds
fat
          in dense
grass

what season
now? brown &
                    brown (translate)
dull silver:
          nickels of rain
startle our dust   our house
shudders,
          rusts

                bicycle
broom

I had my own room
in the old house   blown
now
                    set
at brick's edge

                              how

small dog & shoes

            to lose already
the white thread
            the blue—
mother's hue (pink rose)
                    & father
        sows
                          stars

yellow as corn
between born-at-night
       green—

remind me again:
there was a great storm.
fate & character,
       the warm straw
in which to sleep

to dream

a dress, a table-
       cloth—spotted wash

(knew not this
pink   apple blossom
       gossamer
more than spun—
         strung
filament   thin
    as kisses)

our year   a night
steeped—   straw thru seams
        we wandered:
slight stars.   a basket
of grass   our task
        of sleep

bicycle, broom

        a man selling
potions in poor
rooms   up &
        down
county—reckon he
won't hurt none & might
        cure some   one

hogs &
       cloud breaks—
raked sky fallow
for a song.
       long news across the grass:

under house
a woman   curls
&   disappears

           I inherit
     her shoes

(in exact language)

ruby, red, rouge
      (translate, please)

& mother lost before
the storm: corn &
dust

     disease

burlap   crows
     I loved a man
leaky, unsewn
          mended him with
song & such thread as could be
found—

the path you depart from is not the way
which is to say   we met
another man of metal
          skin—thin timbered
out of sorts (just like someone I knew
back home)
                    some things I can't re-
member
                    some I chop down at night &
          wake to find full-grown

again—

a woodsman without woods
or blood to call his own:
some say   soldiers
blown for fields come home
without complete   machinery

          their hearts' compart-
ments empty &   unoiled—

he toiled with an axe
abandoned by his maker

translate home:
          heart, brain, basket
of fur, the soul's trim
flame calibrated
to stir the evening air.
                              radio. clothesline.
          voices. time.

                    a little dog

a big tom-
cat of a man
worn   as old corduroy.
no boy I knew was ever so
          soft.   growling,
purring: the whir of a motor
                    under my hand

no metaphor:
the war that's coming

       dance music
on the radio—summer dust
blows
           trickles
under sill—
fills the house up   while
    we listen

patched men,
      my friends—
we sleep by the side
of the road.
I'm a bride strung
      with poppies. cat,
straw, tin—a thin
snow begins to fall.
        somewhere
our work is being done:
      bales stacked &
water poured
floor swept
        hours   mended

listen—green husks
sizzle in the wind. a little
silk   gilds the sound:
          big round kernels
of gold.
          little emerald—
          I climb your stem's thick
                              rungs

her face is also green
          that other—
I know I didn't dream it.

her crystal screens a voice
which seeks me. mother, why
bear & name & leave
          to other's calling?

her image stalls, can't be refreshed:

          auntie's shapeless
                    hands, her soft
          dress

brothers, lovers:
        in the hog pen squeals
at feed time—mud
revels.

time's reel
        squeaks along—a rag
a myth   of pigs & men
        & poppy fields—

        insistent music:
ache of shoes designed
for dancing.   context =
sex of the farm—warm weather
        ruts & shudders:
        piglets
fresh milk

a witch   is a woman
        of wax
spilling my name
in the sky
        a dry wick
kindled
into flame.
                    & I?

I have nothing
but fear—
            sere windburnt land.
tin hand, straw breast, a thin
upholstery of need.

        this is chiefly an account of sleep
& faith—a small house lit
in the landscape—a wraith of hearth-
smoke seen from the road.
                    & years—

(but everything had a name
        already—
am I to blame for these   wishes?)

The Orange Window

for Carmina

What will die with me when I die, what pathetic
or fragile form will the world lose? The voice of
Macedonio Fernández, the image of a red horse
in the vacant lot at Serrano and Charcas, a bar of
sulphur in the drawer of a mahogany desk?
—JORGE LUIS BORGES, "The Witness"

The Whale

I woke, chased the receding tide of dreams, then woke fully, already in open sea. It was hot and I remembered Anna waking, stepping out onto the platform, where snow began to fall. My plush delight at her stolen lover, his strained face. The billowing steam of their train beneath the Russian night I spangled richly with my own familiar stars.

The Reins

He dipped his bread, bit into it lavishly, with the free gesture of a son at his mother's table. The massive mammal had wandered in from the sea, up the broad thigh of a salt river. "Descended from a cow," he said, with a certain pleasure. I sipped my wine, no longer cold. He saw her from a train, surrounded by men on horseback, and thought of jumping. "Not to save her from slaughter, which would have been impossible," he looked down into the little cast iron pot. "Perhaps to look into her eye."

The Caldron

The sea was not as I had imagined it would be. It was smoother, like a rumpled blanket. I was pleasantly bored, sometimes restless; at night I seemed to roll lightly through borrowed dreams. I experimented with my food and drink, eating only shellfish one day, drinking only mineral water the next. I observed my fellow passengers in some detail, particularly the German family with their sunshades at noon. The daughter wore a ribbon around her neck at dinner: black velvet, tied at the back, no doubt by her mother's hands.

Agustín de Vedia

I sat at the head of the table where my father must have sat. His tinted portrait watched us every night, silently eating the food she had cooked that afternoon. I'm ashamed to say how little I remember of that time, those dishes; I was perpetually pushing my chair back, eager for my books, my puddle of lamplight.

Library

In those days it was not uncommon to retrieve a dream whole to the shores of waking. I caught several in the span of a single lush and undecided winter. Winds rattled the glass, desiccated my nose and mouth. A man in a short jacket handed me a sheaf of white pages. An untitled work, beginning with the number 3, firmly and exactly inked.

Bread

At about this time I befriended the clock. His fatherly aspect soothed my passage through the hours. Unquestionably, I sought my own reflection in his visage, and found it when the light sufficed. I: heavy lids, full mouth, two punctuating nostrils. Bordered by his perfect sphere, swept by his delicate arm with its golden arrow. I confess to napping in the afternoons simply to arrange him beside me on the pillow and doze under his gentle gaze. It was during one of these naps that I first dreamt of the library.

Orthography

M was impatient with my research and my distraction, which he considered inextricably linked. My offering of a slab of buckwheat honeycomb only sweetened his diatribe, as he sucked the chambers and chewed their wax. We agreed I would present my research at month's end without fail. On my way home, stopping before a window to consider a pair of lilac gloves, I saw her reflected, exiting a shop across the street, on another man's arm. The lilies in her free hand caught the light, momentarily illuminating my own face in the milliner's glass.

Manuscript

It wasn't filled with books, per se, or at least not ordinary volumes. Rather, it was populated with innumerable presences, radiant masses of light and dust, each emitting its own frequency and taking shape under the reader's eye. Whirlwind, ladder, a woman's torso, a galloping horse; all composed of glittering particles animated by an unseen force into constant motion. Surprisingly, I felt no desire to touch these magical books, and no impulse to analyze them. My pleasure and absorption were complete as I stood in their peripheries, reading.

Spoons

"I have lived in this little town all my life, with my deaf brother to look after. We walk together in the dusk, season after season. Does time pass? Children pass us but no longer squander their laughter on our progress to the cinema or the bakery. My brother works in the evening at his great project: a text of all the films we have seen. Perhaps you imagine a screenplay, or the flat script of subtitles, but you are wrong. At our kitchen table he weaves scene and character, plot and movement. Every cut is described by his text, every change of light. All that is missing are the words and music. These you must complete in your mind. Please respond to the address below, if you would be interested in translating such a manuscript."

Parenthesis

M was late, which surprised me. I ordered another brandy and unfolded my newspaper. The sense of being mistaken in our plan began to steal over me. I pictured him sitting at El Sueño, beginning a second brandy of his own, and fingering the soft weight of dusty newsprint. Was he seeing the same woman's shoulders at the next table? Or another's, her sister perhaps, waiting for a gentleman of good reputation and familiar cigars. My watch tingled a bit. Looking down again, I read that a new planet had been discovered, that a boy had been kidnapped, that the estate sale of X would begin tomorrow at noon.

26 Avenida Descansada

The room's painted walls were perpetually wet, which seemed strangely appropriate to me. Of course, in moving about, my sleeve might graze those surfaces. I worried a bit at first, until it became clear that I would rub off on them, rather than the reverse. Soon the room was gently scarred with my traces. These abrasions had the quality of a changing sky: each one seemed to reflect my mood at our point of contact. A rosy welter from yesterday morning, when I was looking forward to a certain appointment; thin streaks of lead on my return, when I was so absorbed in revisiting each word spoken, with mounting regret, that my brush against the door frame went completely unnoticed.

Honor

"Titles, light as butterflies, or minnows rising in a wavelet. Successive, several at a time, diminishing to one, the most important. Always a man's name, in Italian, French or English. His signature. A breath."

El Sueño

First the lighter household goods: linens, embroidered drapes, an enormous array of parasols and sunshades. Then imported porcelain, heavy silver and pewter, the quaint wooden kitchen tools, a coffee grinder, a set of exquisite knives. Furniture, dolls, playing cards, writing accoutrements which I resisted with difficulty. A saber from some forgotten war, purchased reverentially by a man who might have used it himself. Oval mirrors for man and wife. Intricate personal effects: jewelry, watches, decorative combs. Tinted photographs in chipped fames. But no books, not even a bible.

Alexandria

M's intentions were excellent, he assured me. "But one must proceed in these matters with the utmost caution. Lonely women, isolated from the world, must be treated delicately. Their minds have developed in a kind of vortex, which gives way to the most exaggerated notions of romance at the least word from a stranger. But, of course, you know this already," he smiled, depositing an olive pit in his palm.

Compass

"Spatters of light coming into focus: a city street lit by night. A white cigarette, a supple line. His broad back dimly haloed. A sense of counting."

Scene

By accident, I discovered his small package, returned for lack of postage. Homely and intriguing, it sat on his doorstep with script crawling across its immaculate label. An extra flourish in her final consonant. Giving a last unhopeful knock I turned back into the alley, cooling now in the late afternoon.

Cinema

Whatever I felt in those first days is lost to me now. I can only remember little fish skittering near shore, the low boats melting into dusky glints at sunset. So many old men playing cards in the open cafes. And myself, wandering that harbor with a small book in my pocket, looking up from my feet at each person who passed. Everyone looked old to me there, even the children screaming past with their monstrous sea treasures. At night I dreamt my mother walked toward me in a white dress, calmly, with a resolve that was never hers in life.

Las Brisas

M went to great lengths to hide his obsession. He borrowed my botanical books and *The Questions of Zaran* along with several volumes of sonnets, in an amusing effort to throw me off the scent. His quickened steps down the alley, across two squares lit with flowers, and down the palm-lined boulevard to the post office became an almost daily event. Still, he lingered at the edge of El Sueño's mosaic tile every evening, engrossed in The Sixth Question, or The Seventh, sipping sherry and tugging at his moustache.

The Skein

"You are so kind with your letters. I particularly appreciated your parcel of June 27; it restored to me a poem I loved as a young girl. The preserves are unlike anything we've ever tasted and I hope you don't mind my sharing them with my brother. His sense of taste is remarkably developed, and he said the fruit enabled him to envision your town with its bright window frames and warm breezes. I'm enclosing a local sweet, *marrons glacés*. I hope their ancient recipe conveys a graceful arc, a phrase of melody…"

Newspaper

I was unable to learn the native card game, though I tried for three nights. It was this failing that secured my place in the village: that of lovable imbecile. Everywhere I went, people smiled at me as though we shared a common joke. I was invited home to dinners of fish head soup and rough hard bread, to join in evening promenades, to hold the raveled end of a net being mended. I was clapped on the back. Certain words became known to me through repetition, and I wrote them in the back cover of my book. I began to consider staying in that seaside pocket where the women wore white blouses and smiled behind their laundry lines.

Absolute

Her face had turned to stone, slowly and abruptly at the same time. Rivulets of water left a salt signature, white against marbled charcoal. Lying beside her, I waited for the inevitable horsemen and looked up at our sky: relentless, familiar, empty.

Las Mujeres

"The Third Question has provided endless fascination for me these past several weeks. Have you considered it? It seems to me that the whole problem lies in Z's conception of language and his attitude toward subjectivity, which he might have been expected to alter with subsequent printings. Nonetheless, I find myself thinking about the intricacies of his logic every moment, sometimes even retracing my steps to test his theories. Have no worries about your house; everything is flourishing. The roses in particular…"

La Ventana

M's translations were laborious and troubled by his lack of affinity for cinema. "I can't understand," he mused, as we paused at his corner, "why anyone would wish to spend an evening, or an afternoon, for God's sake, in a darkened room watching melodrama. And frankly, I'm surprised you disagree with me, given your penchant for the natural world." I could see the crumbling moon reflected in a third-story window above his head, my will to argue dissolving in that humble light.

Translation

The wedding took place one afternoon in late summer. It was an unremarkable day but for that fact; I spent it beside the old wall of the garden. With publication of my bee study had come a flurry of correspondence, which I answered dutifully each week. I heard later that the wedding party had walked from the church to the hall and entered the festooned doorway with a burst of music. Her dress was imported but altered by her two sisters; his hat had belonged to her father. Most of the wine went missing at the beginning and had to be replaced by H, to his great consternation. After dancing for several hours and feeding each other little cakes powdered with sugar, the bridal couple departed to commence their travels. A photograph appeared in our newspaper the following morning; for the first time I noticed how like brother and sister they looked.

Alphabet

"I was troubled by the same concerns; have you reached the end yet? I believe you will be comforted by the last Question, which deals with the residue of experience in terms of obsessive repetition. This he explores in a variety of brilliant ways, my favorite being the streetcar incident. For months I had a recurrent dream about it, which might prove the theory in a single stroke."

Las Blancas

Begun in a lit boat, hot and white on the calm surface. A dark man rowing, his pants clean white, his striped shirt in stark contrast to his russet skin. He worked hard to keep our flat craft in one place, although there was no wind and no land. A ghostly mooring to our right: perhaps fifty boats tied to one another in a grid, perfectly still between the smooth water and the depthless sky. Looking back at my companion, I saw his hands clenched around the oars, knuckles burnt and raveling. Gazing right again, empty sea.

Rio Alejandro

From a silver town three hundred miles north, that simple curl of
leather with its gleaming tongue and punched stars. A
horsewoman's belt, soft and strong, adorned by an old man's
delicate labor in the scorched days of a famous drought. Six-pointed
asterisks to measure her waist. The buckle thin as her pinky. This to
match a pair of boots completed on the last day of rain, which he
had neglected to catch.

The Ditch

The eye inserts a letter, the one that wasn't there. That is our
approach to experience: we seek the expected formation born in
anticipation and upheld by revision. This procedure opposes itself
to the French notion of *depaysment*, in which the traveler is
"uncountried" by discarding the coherent identity he achieves
through a sense of familiar place and culture. Without that
relinquishment, our new perception remains locked in the confines
of what we have already seen, in photographs and films, but
foremost, in our minds.

The Gadfly

M became morose without explanation. Naturally I surmised the cause of his melancholy, but now suspect I was quite wrong. Our meetings became less frequent and were marked by his obsession with the details of his early life, which he now examined solely through the lens of Zaran's Questions. My calm exterior hid a burgeoning sense of betrayal as time passed without his confidence.

The Mine

There was no news of them for some time. In September, a letter to her mother, postmarked Geneva and accompanied by hot dusty winds that surprised the town in its afternoon slumber. Written a full month earlier, her ink had faded to faintest sienna. Her plump vowels and supple linking strokes followed each other in a tilting progress down the page of hotel stationery. Their voyage had been stormy, their debarkation dampened by rain. Seasickness, lost currency, an English novel, the kind ministrations of the Italian stewards. Her scant mention of him gave me grave pleasure as I imagined him searching in vain for the lost billfold.

Election

"So many days have passed without a letter that I begin to worry for your health. If I have offended you in some way, you have my profoundest apology. If you are ill, my heart goes out to you. If the situation is more dire, perhaps my heart will break, so deeply have I come to rely on your friendship."

Arabic

Within the massive, ancient door, a smaller one; designed for a child or dwarf, opened with a tiny key. The night door, allowing my return after evenings at the harbor. Each night I hit my head on its false lintel and swore as I stepped into the dark tiled vestibule which Madame had scrubbed twelve hours before. Then up the crumbling stairs with their scrolled iron railings, to my third floor room. Some nights the little dog would wake and stifle his bark with visible effort. Other nights, a strange song emanated from an interior room on the second floor, and I would pause on the landing, frozen in the mystery of those cries.

Calculus

Without water, dreams stopped. The great ranches, shrouded in dust, came unmoored from their mesas and hovered two stories overhead. Horses grazed the cloudless sky, grew skeletal, shriveled to child-sized husks carried seaward by the bleating wind. On the twenty-sixth day, the old harness-maker lowered himself to earth on a chain wrought of bent iron horseshoes. Tied to his chest, a tiny vial of rainwater with a silver stopper.

Stylus

"Your endeavor continues to impress me and I will certainly send the crate of books immediately. The town news is nothing to speak of, with one exception: young H returned alone two days ago. He went directly to his father's house and hasn't been seen since, despite her family's insistence that they be admitted to the house. Of course I will apprise you of anything I hear."

The Drought

Skirmishes were frequent and momentary. All the boys came from the same neighborhood and looked like twelve brothers. White shirts, disarranged, blue short pants, loose leather sandals which dangled from their languid feet while their colleagues worked problems at the blackboard. The notes passed from their dirty hands became my great amusement in the afternoon, alone in the whitewashed room, still hazy with chalk dust.

Surisa DaConte

Among these things a scrimshaw spoon, no larger that a dragonfly. Its blue markings were Arabic. Originally placed with my other purchases as an afterthought, the spoon began to fascinate as I turned it over under the scientific lamp M had given me. Months would pass before a translating dictionary could be located, but by then the spoon's power had been fully spent.

Sand

Lost in a card game, then won again; jagged on one side, softly worn on the other. I examined it for several seconds, suspended between horror and something approaching mirth. The wonder of its compact weight remained in my palm for hours after I left him. The following day he would be ambushed on the way to the harbor by two rough brothers seeking to avenge their father's humiliation. But that night, as he placed his treasure on the scale pan with delicate long fingers, he had the grace of a northern painting.

The Alphabet

"My brother has taken quite ill. He was often so as a child, and I have many fond memories of tending him through the lesser ailments. Now it is different: he is dark and unpredictable, subject to fits of passionate despair. Two doctors have seen him already and both have recommended a restorative trip to a warmer place. But my brother has never left our village and the idea of moving him fills me with dread."

Aguardiente

Railroad tracks, a gray box hovering above them, interrupting the horizon. Her white dress shimmering. I had walked a great distance; my limbs were luminous with fatigue. She receded from me, walking at a faster pace. I wanted to gallop forward, but stopped instead, where the tracks puckered up from barren sandstone. A trickle of ants labored there, parallel to the iron rail. No two passed without conferring; many carried the bodies of fallen comrades. Looking up, I found myself alone.

Quince

M's correspondence grew thin but then seemed to recover. His intellectual vigor restored, he regaled me with insights about all manner of texts: natural history (in which he had previously deferred to me, with an indulgent smile), metaphysics, and, oddly, certain occult books, which he discussed derisively but in great detail. As my sole connection to the town, he also provided me the local news with its flourishes, disappointments and intrigues. Several young ladies of our acquaintance had recently married. A circus had come and gone. H's grand plan to build a system of aqueducts was publicly ridiculed and abandoned.

Los Arcos

More silver for the jewelry, and nickel for her baggage. Flies circled middle air, lighting sometimes on the pile of Venetian lace. The dog slept in a tiled shadow, his nostrils flaring wetly as he snored. She herself lay nearby, stroking a path between squares with her thumb.

The Queen of Wands

I began to yearn for my study. Without cicadas, night came too quickly, and I paced my room in consternation, unable to embark on another evening. My few things clung to the room accusingly. In the study my father's desk gleamed dark as a coffin. Paperweights glimmered with watery light, the smooth amber pieces glowed hotly. In that room a distinctive fragrance, as of an ancient spice. Secretly I thought of it as the breath of my books, exhaled by night as their contents churned and stuttered. Stepping into sea air, I resolved to arrange my passage.

The Slate

The loss of her corporeal self was less surprising than the feeling that accompanied it: a sudden overwhelming heaviness. From her formidable feminine height she tumbled under the weight of the air, crouched compact in the wet grass, or rather in the spaces between the blades. The grass was foreign, soft and bright, completely unlike the wiregrass of her childhood. Under it, a mattress of black earth. She imagined sinking until she emerged on the other side of the world, in white sand, or out of the violet-streaked mesa outside her mother's window.

El Escritorio

M's trips to the post office ceased, as did his frequent book borrowing. Yet his high spirits persisted, marked as always by the gay impatience and curiosity I had come to expect from him. That autumn we dined together often, and he surprised me with a homemade cake on my birthday. Between rum-soaked mouthfuls we debated the last Question, which continued to trouble him despite my efforts to illuminate Zaran's argument with examples from my own experience. "No, I simply can't agree with you," he said, laying down his fork, "although I grasp the elegance of your argument quite clearly. The collapsibility of time is so crucial to the Question that it can't be ignored by your father's umbrella. You must find another way to convince me, and I don't think you you'll be able to."

Latin

"We are three days from shore and I find myself enchanted by this floating life: our daily routines seem elemental and unhurried in a way they never did at home. My brother is much cheered by the expanse of air and the water, which he watches almost without ceasing. Yesterday there was a great commotion due to the discovery of a young stowaway who was at last identified as the steward's daughter. Evidently her mother died recently and the man had no family to lodge her. She couldn't be more than eight or nine, with long plaits and black eyes. Our fellow passengers have talked of little else since she emerged sleepily from a lifeboat and began searching for her father."

The Blackboard

But most of all, the hours, which I desired more than anything else, to pursue my studies and the dreams which seemed to increase in number every night. Those must be diminished as my mother's estate dwindled and finally disappeared. The solicitor's crisp envelope lay on the desk with the rest of the mail M had gathered in my absence. How often had I opened his correspondence casually, or even with vague annoyance, and placed the thin check in my book for deposit! Everything was as I had remembered it, with one exception: the dark study was completely without fragrance.

The Southern Clouds

I amused myself by reorganizing the garden along the new principles I had witnessed abroad, which I hoped would yield magnificent results in the spring. Cold early light poured around my hands and brightened them against the brick-colored clods I piled and crumbled. In the interstices of this work I rested in the wooden swing and read the new Quain volume, which M had kindly left on my desk. The first three days passed in this manner, without a single interruption; on the fourth, young H's hat appeared above the old wall, its smooth pelt a bit rough around the brim.

Bernardo Juan Francisco

"Soon we will be there, in the town we have imagined for so long. My brother's transformation is quite remarkable; I don't remember him ever so animated, even in childhood. He has bet me a glass of local spirits he'll be the first to sight land, and I expect to pay that debt very soon. My heart flies ahead of me…"

blaue augen

for Edward

the barbarian's color

by misdividing the initial
together with the article

                               glazed and painted
                               Spanish-speaking

        Where is?

                   cut from this mineral

                                       the clear cloudless

sky

a lesson on

       that bow or arc

heavens opposite

      Italian paper, her watery fingers
      unfold and refold

           afternoon bells

standard in book painting

(berries

blood

I have left the other
under winter drops

whoever is a weaver

may put another in his place

under the eye

certain hours

then the river is reddened

(by scratching
in painted walls
in certain margins

brazilwood

        saffron

India stone

handfuls of these blossoms from our roof
and the tiny whites for dolls

bent by drowning

        the flowers here are moon-colored

        pearly head heavy

        lifted

            for a moment

the color of foolishness

(surgeons, executioners,

prostitutes
                    minstrels

                              the legs are white

                              having no idea of sky

blue tales
blau sein
blue hour
blue devils

                              (and sometimes women

It was

                  for me

                                    my simple

in which

                            becoming

        exactly   *one*

                         another

                blue

(still now

some thousand dresses

bare flutes

chromophilia

the sketch underneath   azurite:

used for centuries

by Italians before Northern

pinks and oranges

(what spills
expensive

(especially for skies

the breast's wet

paper

blaue augen

some turning–

Frou-Frou, Frou-Frou

victrola's guarded flower

aerial views

petaled officer

grey smudged incantation   earth hue missing

to shoot down, to capture

to feed   another language

contours

a form of artifice

music stains the streets

stains

the retreat of red

il me plaît

avec les yeux bleus

wine over potatoes

a man with rabbits

a man who loves clothes

afraid to burn his hands

(moustache

socks

a woman's boots beside the door

if not black

an empty square at the middle

flesh-touched edge

spelling

spills the mouth

little stumps of indigo

snap

the way a man walks

        if the building has eyes

midnight rounds

        in the hue:

a brothel will uncrease your trousers   *unshine your shoes*

    oyster girls

      a hat   for unplanned losses

the miraculous draft of fishes

cerulean:

a tile knocked loose

unseats your autumn

some years slipped

asleep beside stitches

and under yellow

carved coordinates

a lettered globe:

facets

opening

appetite

partitioned sky

all day

in the mouth

stratus

whether a woman

                strung to fitting stars

divides into quarters

her stain slips out of mouth

across sleeping

              ocean

roof tops   drops
                              of gold

a few names flag   green:

these are just   pictures

casual statues

man and horse

sand

leaves

            birds are hidden in short
conical trees

planets   trim the window

whir of   tiny bones   a few
musicians

and that one with his   collar
                        and bell

            (and the lettered border of her dress

of soft seeming stone

eye's erosion

time's uneven stitch:

                         men of ash

gold starred

       betweens

when an angel comes

summing   deed and letter

breadcrumbs in the trees

a scattering—

woman of the pregnant   book

                              pages swollen

by your eyes

celadon
cobalt
azure
bronze

sun's money

sea's dark

    skin

(the invitation to dream
dyed with indigo
boat sails
miners, workers, slaves

attached by rivers
    to the sky

Notes

"The Orange Window":
Many of the titles come from the Borges story "Funes the
Memorious" in the *Labyrinths* translation.

"blaue augen":
The title of this section comes from the film *Grand Illusion*,
Jean Renoir, director. This writing came about through reading
Michel Pastoureau's magnificent book *Blue, The History of a Color*.

PHOTO: ANNA QUINTERO RUIZ

VALERIE COULTON'S work has appeared in *New American Writing, Bird Dog, Big Ugly Review, Parthenon West Review, 26,* and others. Her books include *passing world pictures* (chapbook), EtherDome Press, 2002, *passing world pictures* (full-length version), Apogee Press, 2003, and *the lily book* (winner of the Michael Rubin Chapbook Award), San Francisco State University Press, 2004.

TITLES FROM APOGEE PRESS

TO ORDER OR FOR MORE INFORMATION GO TO
WWW.APOGEEPRESS.COM